DEMCO

Once There Was a Caterpillar

For Meriel - J.A.

For Hannah, Carl, Heather,
and little miss trouble! - M.G.

First edition for the United States, its territories and
dependencies, and Canada published in 2010 by
Barron's Educational Series, Inc.

First published in 2009 by Wayland
Copyright © Wayland 2009

Wayland
338 Euston Road, London, NW1 3BH

All inquiries should be addressed to:
Barron's Educational Series, Inc.
250 Wireless Boulevard, Hauppauge, NY 11788
www.barronseduc.com

The right of Judith Anderson to be identified as the author
of the work has been asserted by her in accordance with
the Copyright, Designs, and Patents Act 1988.

Editor: Nicole Edwards • Designer: Paul Cherrill
Digital Color: Carl Gordon

Library of Congress Control Number: 2009933528

ISBN-13: 978-0-7641-4494-3
ISBN-10: 0-7641-4494-4

Date of Manufacture: December 2009
Manufactured by: WKT, Shenzhen, China

Printed in China
9 8 7 6 5 4 3 2 1

Nature's Miracles

Once There Was a
Caterpillar

Written by
Judith Anderson

Illustrated by
Mike Gordon

Caterpillars are amazing!
Some are hairy. Some have
spots or stripes.

4

And some of them live in
my mom's cabbage patch.

5

A caterpillar starts out as a tiny egg.

Cool!

6

These eggs are stuck to this leaf. They can't fall off.

Look!

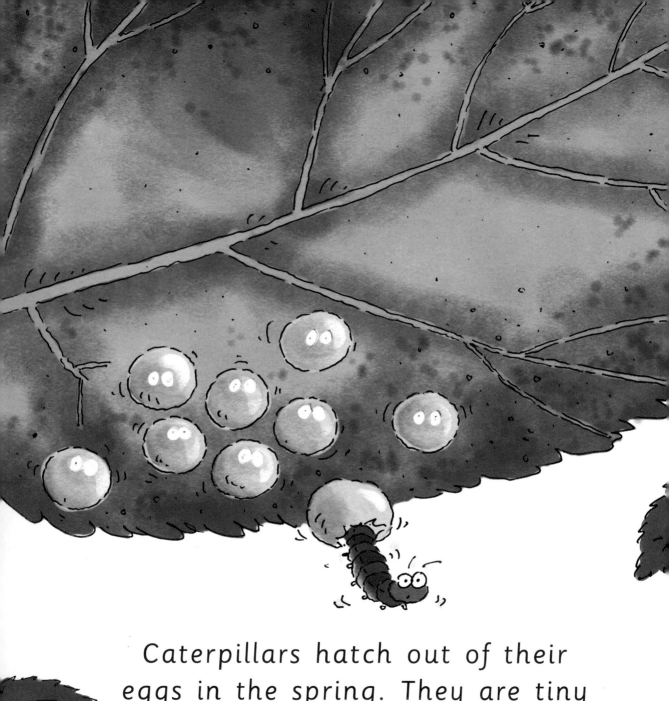

Caterpillars hatch out of their
eggs in the spring. They are tiny
and very hungry.

They start to eat right away.
Leaves are their favorite food.
In fact, leaves are their only food!

As they eat,
they grow.

10

They grow so quickly that they soon grow out of their skin.

Luckily, new skin has already grown underneath the old skin.

This happens quite a few times!

I've grown, too!

By the end of summer,
the caterpillars have
grown big and fat.

But they don't stay caterpillars forever. They change.

Time to go!

First, they shed
their skin one last
time. Then, they
attach themselves
to a nice leaf or twig.

Next, they make a hard shell to protect themselves. This is called a chrysalis. The chrysalis looks just like another leaf or twig.

Safe inside the chrysalis, the caterpillar starts to change. Now it is called a pupa.

It loses its fat body and starts to grow long legs and wings.

This change is called metamorphosis.

Then, when the pupa is ready, it breaks out of the chrysalis.

But it isn't a pupa anymore.
The pupa has become a
beautiful butterfly.

The butterfly warms
itself in the sun.
Then it flies off to
look for food.

Butterflies don't eat leaves. They drink sweet nectar from flowers.

That's not the end
of the story, though.

After the winter, the female butterfly returns to the same kind of plant or tree from where it first hatched.

It lays some new eggs
on a leaf, and soon these
eggs hatch into a new
family of caterpillars.

So the caterpillar's story starts all over again. It is called a "life cycle" because it goes around and around.

NOTES FOR PARENTS AND TEACHERS

Suggestions for reading the book with children

As you read this book with children, you may find it helpful to stop and discuss what is happening page by page. Children might like to talk about what the pictures show, and point out the changes taking place in the young caterpillar.

The idea of a life cycle is developed throughout the book, and reinforced on the final pages with the diagram of the eggs, caterpillar, chrysalis, and butterfly. Ask the children if they know of any other life cycles. Can they see any patterns in nature? The other titles in this series may help them think about this.

Discussing the subject of caterpillars and butterflies may introduce children to a number of unfamiliar words, including chrysalis, pupa, hatch, nectar, and metamorphosis. Make a list of new words and discuss what they mean.

Nature's Miracles

There are four titles about life cycles in the **Nature's Miracles** series: *Once There Was a Seed; Once There Was a Caterpillar; Once There Was a Tadpole;* and *Once There Was a Raindrop.* Each book encourages children to explore the natural world for themselves through direct observation and specific activities and emphasizes developing a sense of responsibility toward plants, animals, and natural resources.

Once There Was a Caterpillar will help young readers think about how caterpillars and butterflies are part of the world around them. The book also provides learning and discussion by introducing children to the idea that caterpillars and butterflies require specific conditions and adaptations for survival.

Suggestions for follow-up activities

The children in this book discover that some caterpillars and butterflies like cabbages best. If you want to attract a wide variety of caterpillars and butterflies into a garden or playground, talk to the children about how different species lay their eggs and feed on different plants, and try growing some of their favorites such as nasturtiums, lavender, and honesty. Buddleia will also attract many species of butterfly.

Remember, too, that butterflies need shelter and warmth in addition to food. If you are making a butterfly garden, choose a sunny spot, out of the wind, and check that there is a source of water from a puddle or shallow dish set into the soil. Some species also like rotting fruit such as apples or pears.

Alternatively, try looking for caterpillars and butterflies in wild areas, as several common species favor nettles, thistles, or ragwort. Encourage the children to write down the names of the insects they see and the plants on which they find them. Do, however, remind the children that nettles and thistles will sting and prickle if touched!

31

Books to read

The Very Hungry Caterpillar by Eric Carle (Puffin, 2002)
Why Should I Protect Nature? by Jen Green, illustrated by Mike Gordon (Barron's Educational Series, Inc., 2005)

Useful websites

www.kidzone.ws/animals/butterflypics/monarchpicstory.html
www.tooter4kids.com/LifeCycle/Butterfly_Life_Cycle.htm
www.encyclopedia.com/topic/caterpillar.aspx
http://en.wikipedia.org/wiki/Caterpillar

Index